I0813329

WELCOME TO
SINGAPORE
COUNTRIES OF THE WORLD
Singapore
by Suzane Nguyen
BLASTOFF!
2
READERS
BLASTOFF! READERS, AN IMPRINT OF BELLWETHER MEDIA BY FLUTTERBEE

Blastoff! Readers are carefully developed by literacy experts to build reading stamina and move students toward fluency by combining standards-based content with developmentally appropriate text.

Level 1 provides the most support through repetition of high-frequency words, light text, predictable sentence patterns, and strong visual support.

Level 2 offers early readers a bit more challenge through varied sentences, increased text load, and text-supportive special features.

Level 3 advances early-fluent readers toward fluency through increased text load, less reliance on photos, advancing concepts, longer sentences, and more complex special features.

★ **Blastoff! Universe**

Reading Level

Grade K

Grades 1–3

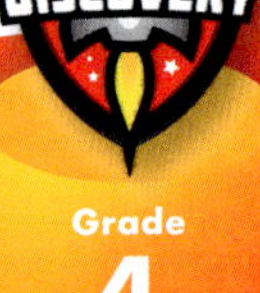

Grade 4

This edition first published in 2026 by Bellwether Media, Inc.

For information regarding permission, write to Bellwether Media, Inc., Attention: Permissions Department, 3500 American Blvd W, Suite 150, Bloomington, MN 55431.

Library of Congress Cataloging-in-Publication Data is available at www.loc.gov or upon request from the publisher.

Names: Nguyen, Suzane, author.
Title: Singapore / by Suzane Nguyen.
Description: Minneapolis, Minnesota : Bellwether Media, Inc., 2026. | Series: Countries of the world | Includes bibliographical references and index. | Audience: Ages 5-8 | Audience: Grades 2-3 | Summary: "Relevant images match informative text in this introduction to Singapore. Intended for students in kindergarten through third grade"-- Provided by publisher.
Identifiers: LCCN 2025042152 (print) | LCCN 2025042153 (ebook) | ISBN 9798893047875 (hardcover) | ISBN 9798893048872 (ebook)
Subjects: LCSH: Singapore--Juvenile literature.
Classification: LCC DS609 .N48 2026 (print) | LCC DS609 (ebook)
LC record available at https://lccn.loc.gov/2025042152
LC ebook record available at https://lccn.loc.gov/2025042153)

Editor: Ashley Kuehl Designer: Brittany McIntosh

Printed in the United States of America, North Mankato, MN.

Table of Contents

All About Singapore

Singapore

Singapore is a small country in Southeast Asia. It is south of the Malay **Peninsula**.

The capital of Singapore is also Singapore.

Land and Animals

Singapore is made up of one big island and around 60 smaller islands.

The country is mostly flat. The eastern part is a **plateau**. The western and southern parts have **cliffs**.

Bukit Timah Hill

Size: 537 feet (164 meters) tall

Famous For: highest point in Singapore

Singapore is a **tropical** country.
It is hot most of the year.

Monsoons happen in the winter and summer. They bring wind and rain.

Most animals live in **nature reserves**. Monkeys swing from treetops. Lorises eat fruit from branches.

long-tailed macaque

Birds peck at ants. Snakes move along the **rainforest** floor.

Life in Singapore

Singapore is **diverse**. Most Singaporeans have a Chinese **background**. There are four official languages.

Most Singaporeans live in the city.

English: Hello
Mandarin: ni hao
(nee-HAOW)

soccer

mah-jongg

Soccer is a popular sport.
Many adults play mah-jongg.

Singaporeans go to **festivals**. There are festivals for art, music, and more!

Chicken rice is chicken cooked in hot liquid. *Roti prata* is a flatbread.

Singaporean Food

chicken rice

roti prata

kaya toast

chendol

Kaya toast has coconut jam and butter. *Chendol* is shaved ice topped with jelly!

Chinese New Year happens early in the year. People wear red and light fireworks.

Chinese New Year

Families gather for Diwali. People decorate their homes with oil lamps. It is a festival of lights!

Singapore Facts

Size:
278 square miles
(719 square kilometers)

Population:
6,028,459 (2024)

National Holiday:
National Day (August 9)

Main Languages:
English, Mandarin, Malay, Tamil

Capital City:
Singapore

Famous Face

Name: Jeanette Aw

Famous For: actor and businessperson

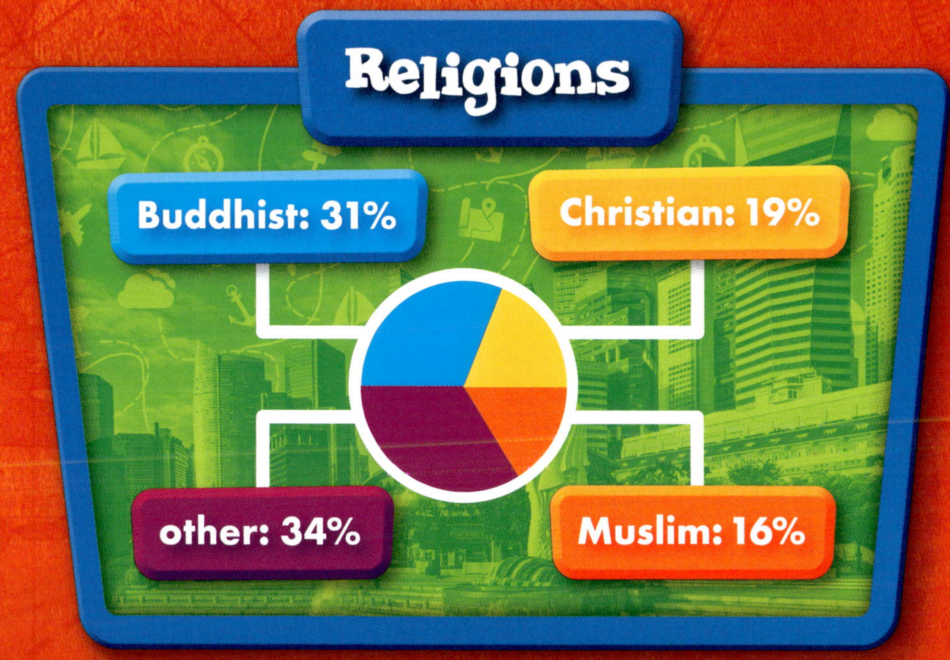

Top Landmarks

Bukit Timah Nature Reserve

Gardens by the Bay

Merlion Park

Glossary

background—a person's experiences, knowledge, and family history

cliffs—high, steep surfaces of rock, earth, or ice

diverse—made up of people whose backgrounds or identities are different from one another

festivals—times or events of celebration

monsoons—winds that change direction each season; monsoons can bring heavy rain.

nature reserves—areas of nature where animals and plants are protected

peninsula—a section of land that sticks out from a larger piece of land and is almost completely surrounded by water

plateau—an area of raised, flat land

rainforest—related to a thick, green forest that receives a lot of rain

tropical—related to a warm place near the equator

AT THE LIBRARY

Gould, Sloan. *Singapore*. New York, N.Y.: Cavendish Square Publishing, 2026.

Phillips-Bartlett, Rebecca. *Chinese New Year*. New York, N.Y.: Greenhaven Publishing, 2023.

Sabelko, Rebecca. *Singapore*. Minneapolis, Minn.: Bellwether Media, 2025.

ON THE WEB

FACTSURFER

Factsurfer.com gives you a safe, fun way to find more information.

1. Go to www.factsurfer.com.
2. Enter "Singapore" into the search box and click 🔍.
3. Select your book cover to see a list of related content.

Index

The images in this book are reproduced through the courtesy of: Perfect Lazybones, front cover; Mini Onion, p. 3; Monticello, pp. 4, 21 (Gardens by the Bay); KTK_Creatives_stockphoto, p. 6; Danny Ye, pp. 6-7; RebekahS, p. 8; Christian Heinz, p. 9; Wirestock Creators, p. 10; Dpongvit, p. 11 (long-tailed macaque); Binturong-tonoscarpe, p. 11 (Sunda slow loris); Martin Pelanek, p. 11 (common flameback); timla wildlife, p. 11 (common wolf snake); Lifestyle Travel Photo, p. 12; Carlina Teteris/ Getty Images, pp. 12-13; Kdonmuang, p. 14 (top); EyeEm Mobile GmbH, p. 14 (bottom); helloitsme_sr, p. 15; Photoongraphy, p. 16 (chicken rice); hhgjhgjh, p. 16 (roti prata); Pyeonan Gallery, p. 16 (kaya toast); Kritchai7752, p. 16 (chendol); kandl stock, p. 17; ROSLAN RAHMAN/ Contributor/ Getty Images, pp. 18-19; Aflo Co. Ltd./ Alamy Stock Photo, p. 20; N8Allen, p. 21 (Bukit Timah Nature Reserve); Majonit, p. 21 (Merlion Park); Kali Justine, p. 23.